THE BEAUTIFUL S
QUENCH

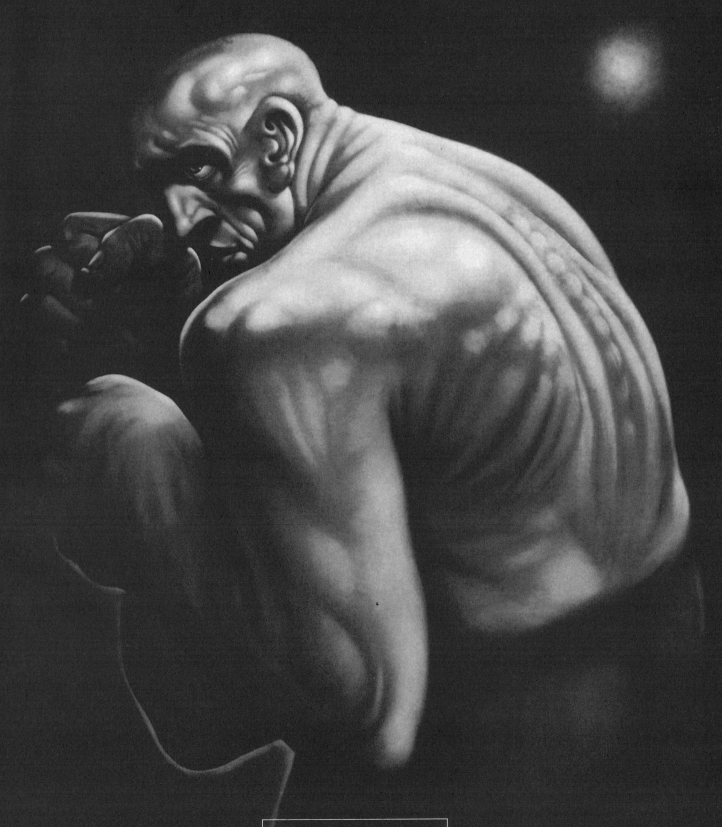

POLYGRAM MUSIC PUBLISHING

HOW LONG'S A TEAR TAKE TO DRY?

Words & Music by Paul Heaton & Dave Rotheray

(Female) 1. How long's a tear— take to dry— when a wo-man has— no—
(Verses 2 & 3 see block lyrics)

—— breeze? How long's a tear— take to dry——

when a wo-man's, when a wo-man's on her knees?

(Male) Look I'm sor-ry that I hurt you, you look a mil-lion dol-lars and a dime.

Time's the great-est heal-er. (F) But

love's the great-est steal-er of all time. (Male) I'm so

To Coda ⊕

clo - ser you are ___ to the grave. ___

D.%. al Coda

⊕ **_Coda_**

(F) How long does sor - ry real - ly last, ___

7

Horns

Verse 2:
(Female)   How long's a tear take to dry
            When a woman hasn't sinned?
            How long's a tear take to dry
            When the weather, when the weather brings no wind?

Verse 3:
(Female)   How long's a tear take to dry
            When almighty brings his rain?
            How long's a tear take to dry
            And do tears, and do tears really stain.

(Male)   This heart was like a tardis
            I went and lost the key in a fight
            I've never found a locksmith
            Will you be my locksmith tonight?
            (Will I shite)

            I'm so sorry *etc.*

THE LURE OF THE SEA

Words & Music by Paul Heaton & Dave Rotheray

♩=104

1. If I walk like a fool___ I've walked like that___ since___ school,
(Verse 2 see block lyric)

but may - be it's the lure of the sea.___

Who knows the ef - fect___ that whis - ky could-'ve had on___ me___

May-be it's the lure of the___ sea,___ may-be it's the lure of the___

___ sea.___ Su-i-cide's just the an - ar-chist that kicks down mo-des - ty,___ but

may - be it's the lure of the sea.___

1.

Maybe it's the lure of the_____ sea,_____

Verse 2:
Once I felt chained, and now, now I feel free
Maybe it's the lure of the sea
Polo and Da Gama
Well those two had nothing on me
Could be I'm a sucker for the sea.

'Cause silver ain't as quick as the tongue
But silver took the M.L.K. so young
And metal ain't as strong as the petal
But metal left the verse unsung.

Maybe it's the lure *etc.*

BIG COIN

Words & Music by Paul Heaton & Dave Rotheray

1. Big coin that you toss for heads or tails,— big coin you let
(Verse 2 see block lyric)

slip down the drain.— Big coin did-n't find— where it land - ed,

big coin,— big coin.— Big coin that you

dropped in the ri - ver, Lit -tle raft— that took you a -cross.—

Lit - tle hand— that pulled it from the gut - ter,

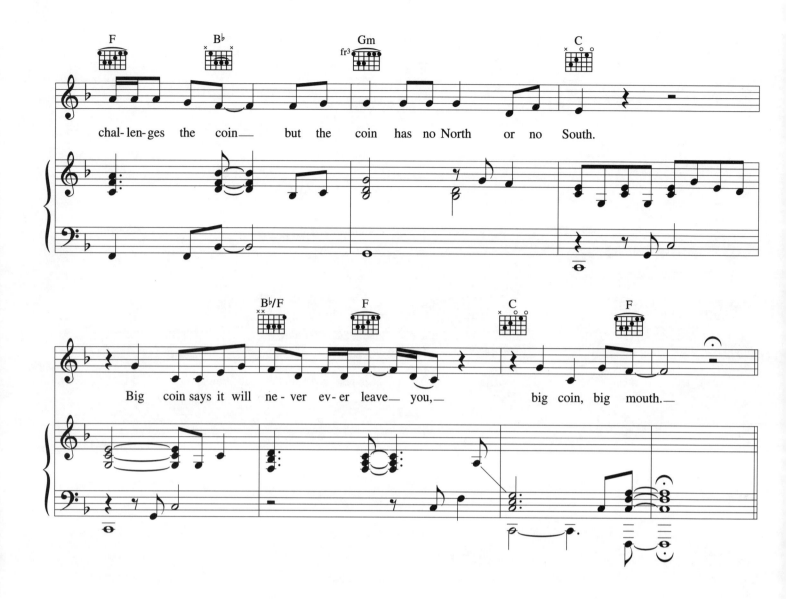

Verse 2:

Big coin that you held and you treasured
Big coin you can't believe that you lost
Little kiss that helped you when you needed
Little kiss, big coin.

Little heart that has no exchange rate
Big coin that could join the I.M.F.
Little heart is only greedy 'cause it's poor
Little heart, big coin.

It's a tiny little heart that challenges the coin
But the coin has no North or no South
Big coin says it will never ever leave you
Big coin, big mouth.

DUMB

Words & Music by Paul Heaton & Dave Rotheray

1. It does-n't take a ma-the-ma-ti-cian
(Verses 2 & 3 see block lyrics)

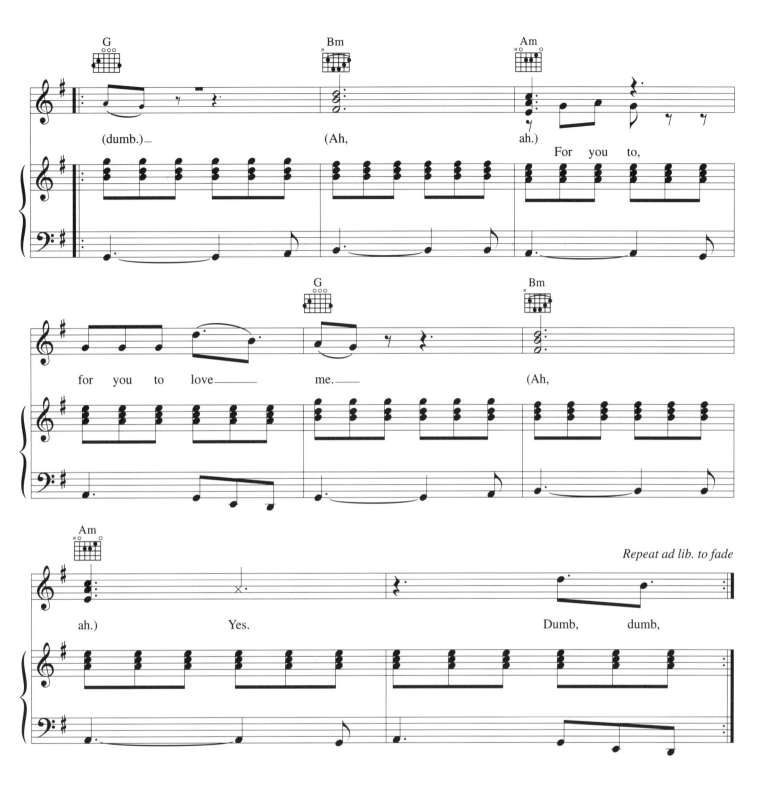

Verse 2:
It doesn't take Robert the Bruce
To see the web you've spun
Either you are simply beautiful
Or I am simply dumb.

Dumb, dumb, dumb *etc.*

Verse 3:
It doesn't take a labrador
To show a blind man sun
Either you are simply beautiful
Or I am simply dumb.

Dumb, dumb, dumb *etc.*

PERFECT 10

Words & Music by Paul Heaton & Dave Rotheray

(Male) 1. She's a per-fect ten—
(Verse 2 see block lyrics)

but she wears a twelve.— Ba-by keep a lit-tle two for me.—

but not on the eyes. _____ Pro - mise me this, ___

take me to - night. _____

(Male) I've bought a watch___ to time your beau - ty

and I've had to fit a se - cond hand. _____

take me to - night._____

'Cos we love our love

Verse 2:

(Female) If he's extra large

Well I'm in charge

I can work this thing on top

And if he's XXL

Well what the hell

Every penny don't fit the slot

(Male) The anorexic chicks

The model six

They don't hold no weight with me

Well eight or nine

Well that's just fine

But I like to hold something I can see.

(Both) 'Cos we love our love *etc.*

THE SLIDE

Words & Music by Paul Heaton & Dave Rotheray

too old for the swings you tend to choose the slide
(Verses 2 & 3 see block lyrics)

1. When you're

and they ne - ver seem to warn you the

slide's your fi - nal ride. And when you're at the top of

it and you can - not see the end,

eith - er don't let go son or grab the near - est friend.

The slide is no_____ re - spect - er_____ of

dig - ni - ty_____ or class._____ As soon as you_____ sit down on

To Coda ⊕

it, that slide has got_____ your ass._____ Don't take the

slide, don't take the_____ slide. He - roes and vil-lains have tried and

cried. A bro-ken soul at the bot-tom lies de - nied. Don't take the

slide, don't take the slide.

1. | 2. D.%. al Coda

2. When the 3. It - 'll

Coda

slide, don't take the slide. He - roes and vil-lains have tried and

cried, a pile of bro-ken souls at the bot-tom it de-nied. Don't take the

slide.— Don't take the slide,— don't take the slide.—

Verse 2:
When the slide was invented
A thousand drinkers sighed
They thought they had the copyright
On the very word the slide
It's a picture of innocence
On which the innocent have fried
Take the helter skelter son
It's easier than the slide
Advice to listening parents
Or the father of the bride
Let them marry anyone
But don't let her take the slide.

Don't take the slide *etc.*

Verse 3:
It'll take you much, much lower
Than you ever would have asked
'Cause as soon as you sit down on it
The slide has got your ass
It's customers are fools
And every one of them deceased
That long and silver murderer
The Devil must have greased
8 bars vocal ad lib.

Don't take the slide *etc.*

LOOK WHAT I FOUND IN MY BEER

Words & Music by Paul Heaton & Dave Rotheray

I can-not steer. Look what I found in my beer.

5. Look what we found in the dance,

look what we've found in the song,

low ex-pec-ta-tions and a large pile of cans. It makes the drink seem weak,

Verse 3:
Look what I found in my drink
A brain without a plughole and a sink without a think
Look what I found in my drink
A "Love you" to the barmaid and a too-familiar wink.

Verse 4:
Look what we found in his booze
The reflection of him and his children without shoes
Look what we found in his booze
This morning's jigsaw in a hill of last nights clues.

Look what I found in the drum *etc.*

THE TABLE

Words & Music by Paul Heaton & Dave Rotheray

1. This

ta - ble has four sturdy legs,___ a heart of ve-ry near_ wild

(Verse 2 see block lyric)

oak. When oth-ers would have screamed out loud, my friend,___

this one ne-ver ev - en spoke.___ I've been sat up-on, ooh,___ I've been

spat up-on, ooh.___ I've been treat-ed like a bed, been car-ried like a stretch-er when some-

48

Verse 2:
This table's been pushed against the door
When tempers, well tempers flare at night
Banged upon with knuckles clenched my friend
When someone thinks that they are right.

I've been sat upon *etc.*

WINDOW SHOPPING FOR BLINDS

Words & Music by Paul Heaton & Dave Rotheray

(Male) 1. One day I'm load-ed, next day I'm broke. Spent all my mo-ney on
(Verse 2 see block lyric)

whis-ky and coke. Rid-ing high____ till the rock hit the spoke, it's like

doors are shut on us, the ne-on lights fa-ded to grey.___ They

say I drink too much, to me, well that's just pro-found.___

How do you know you can't swim un-til you have drowned? Well there's

al-ways a drop in the bot-tle, la-dy, al-ways a sip of the wine.

The glass does-n't seem___ quite___ so emp-ty when

win - dow shop-ping for blinds.___ *(Female)* It's like gate - crash - ing a field,

(Male) that's not true, they've a har - vest they yield. Save your tears for your

1.

eve - 'ning- meal, when you're win - dow shop-ping for blinds.

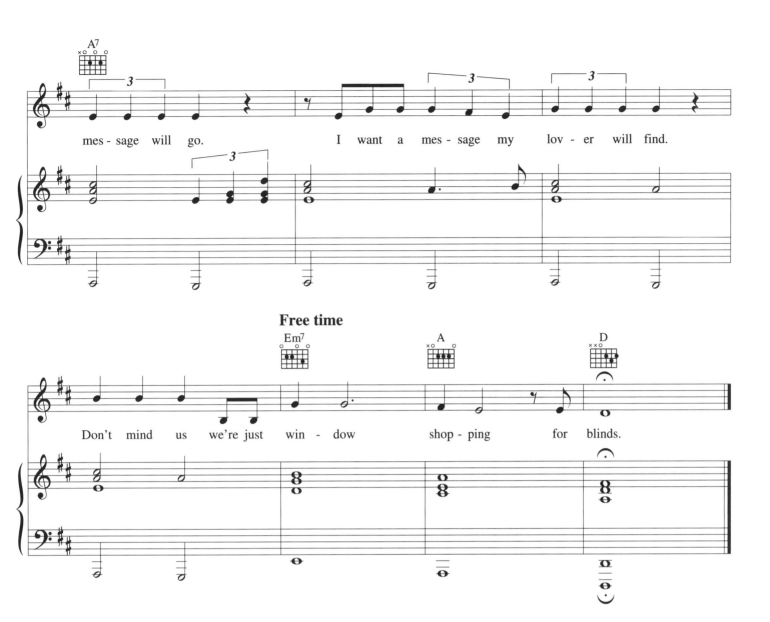

Verse 2:

(Male) One day you're sober, the next day you're not
One day you're remembered, the next day forgot
Spent all my money on cocaine and pot
It's like window shopping for blinds.

(Female) Covered in bruises from head to toe
No-one to speak to and nowhere to go
A map of nowhere and nowhere I know
It's like window shopping for blinds.

(Male & Female) It's like the heartbreak hotel *etc.*

(Female) But what if my husband should come?
(Male) Well tell me what have you done?
You've cherished your vodka, you've cherished your rum
Don't mind us we're just licking our wounds in the sun.

POCKETS

Words & Music by Paul Heaton & Dave Rotheray

© Copyright 1998 Island Music Limited, 47 British Grove, London W4.

be.

2. Here comes

And he's cling-ing on— to hope— like the

oak tree to the gale,_____

'cause

find-ing one love let-ter in a sky-high jum-ble sale_____

Verse 2:
Here comes Pockets
Picking up the things we cannot see
A bicycle, a dame, a Christmas tree
Things of no value to you or me.

Here comes the Pocket
Reduced through history to just a crawl
History turns the tall into the small
But natural born trawlers love to trawl.

And the guitar of his dreams hangs upon some wall
Or laying underneath the staircase in a hall
We can carry dreams but we can't hold them all
That's why we learn the Blues before we actually fall
That's the Pocket, let him be
That's the Pocket, let him be.

LOSING THINGS

Words & Music by Paul Heaton & Dave Rotheray

1. I'm los - ing things,

that's — what old - fa - shioned love brings. — Lost the

key to the house, the feel - ing in my mouth, I'm los — ing things.

2. I'm for - get - ting things, that's — what old -

- fa-shioned love — brings. For - get the num - ber of the street, the

(Verse 3 see block lyric)

know, but so much of me___ don't care.___

I've for -

-got-ten ev-'ry name in my life___ but I still re-mem-ber her.

Oh.___

3. Well I've lost___ her.

Yes,___ yes, yes,___ I'm

lo-sing things.

Yes,___ yes I'm lo-sing things.

Verse 3:
Well I've lost belief
But I've found if you turn that stone
There's love underneath
And when I had belief
I'd spend all my time
Cleaning the grime from my holy teeth

Yes I'm losing things
Yes I'm losing things.

And it's a real Greek Tragedy *etc.*

I MAY BE UGLY

Words & Music by Paul Heaton & Dave Rotheray

1. With a face like a crab's— bus tick-et

(Verse 4 see block lyric)

and skin like a lla-

ash - tray,

it was al - ways gon - na be pan - to -

- mime

that made him sing___ and dance a - ny - way.

When you feel like Lon - don

and you look___ like Hull,

1.

___ you think Tra - vol - ta pulled New - ton - John,___

who did John___ Hurt pull?

4. And he—— sings,   I may be ug - ly,

Verse 4:
And he sings
I may be ugly
But I've got the bottle-opener
He may be fat but he's got the cork-screw
And in the party party politics of the ugly fame
There is no orderly queue.

Verse 5:
And they compliment the compliment
And it's driving you insane
It's like talking to a helicopter
When you know that you're a plane.

Breath like a mountain goat's satchel
Nose like a pool of sick
But you always leave your flies ahoy
'Cause the world wants to suck your dick
Let it suck!

Verse 6:
And he sings I may be ugly
But I've got the bottle-opener
He may may be fat but he's got the cork-screw
And in the party party politics of the ugly fame
There is no, there is no, there is no
There is no orderly queue.

YOUR FATHER AND I

Words & Music by Paul Heaton & Dave Rotheray

(Male) 1. It was the mid-dle of Win-ter, and I drove us in my car.— Well the

snow start-ed fall-ing so we stopped off at a bar.— Well the

(Female 8vb) 2. It was a

hot sum-mer's day____ and we drove there in our car____ and your

(Verse 3 see block lyric)

fath - er was thirs - ty so we had to find a bar.____ Oh, he

would-n't stop drink - ing and he could-n't stand on his feet.____ We had to

pitch black toil-et   in a high-way Ta-co Bell.

(Male) 3. I'll   re - ___

Verse 3:

(*Male*) I'll remember the birth for the rest of my time on this land
Your mother sweating buckets and me holding on to her hand
(*Female*) Well your father was absent, he claimed he couldn't find the ward
Just tugging on mescal, trying to eat the umbilical cord
So if anyone asks you do you know where you're from, say yes
You're from your mother's womb and your father's stinking breath
And if they ask you how you got here, tell them just what it took
Your father's stinking breath and your mother's stinking luck.

Exclusive Distributors:
Music Sales Limited
8/9 Frith Street, London W1V 5TZ,
England.
Music Sales Pty Limited
120 Rothschild Avenue, Rosebery, NSW 2018,
Australia.

Order No. AM954734
ISBN 0-7119-7301-6
This book © Copyright 1998 by
PolyGram Music Publishing.

Music arranged by Derek Jones.
Music processed by Paul Ewers Music Design.
Printed in the United Kingdom by
Caligraving Limited, Thetford, Norfolk.

Your Guarantee of Quality:
As publishers, we strive to produce every
book to the highest commercial standards.
The music has been freshly engraved and,
whilst endeavouring to retain the original
running order of the recorded album,
the book has been carefully designed
to minimise awkward page turns and to
make playing from it a real pleasure.
Particular care has been given to
specifying acid-free, neutral-sized
paper made from pulps which have not
been elemental chlorine bleached.
This pulp is from farmed sustainable
forests and was produced with special
regard for the environment.
Throughout, the printing and binding
have been planned to ensure a sturdy,
attractive publication which should give
years of enjoyment.
If your copy fails to meet our high
standards, please inform us and we will
gladly replace it.

Music Sales' complete catalogue
describes thousands of titles and is available
in full colour sections by subject, direct
from Music Sales Limited.
Please state your areas of interest and send
a cheque/postal order for £1.50 for postage to:
Music Sales Limited, Newmarket Road,
Bury St. Edmunds, Suffolk IP33 3YB.

Visit the Internet Music Shop at
http://www.musicsales.co.uk

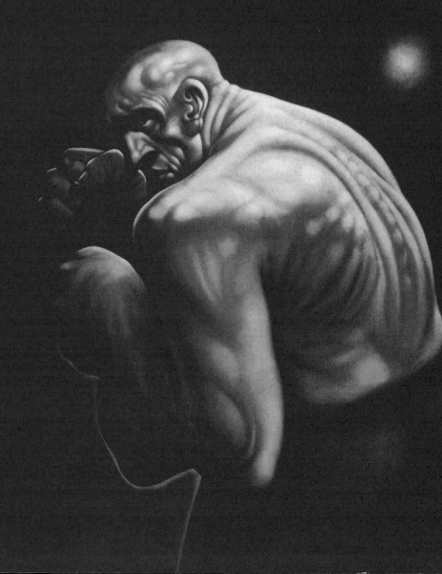